LITTLE JOEY

Goes to Camp

Story by Joe Savalle

Illustrated by Nathan Bortz

ISBN 978-1-7327194-4-6

UNITED HOUSE Publishing
Waterford, Michigan
info@unitedhousepublishing.com
www.unitedhousepublishing.com

Cover art and design, interior illustrations and design: Nathan Bortz
Joe Savalle bio photo: Dream Out Loud Media
Nathan Bortz bio photo: Rina Gholson

Published in Waterford, MI
Printed in the United States

2019—First Edition

SPECIAL SALES
Most UNITED HOUSE books are available at special quantity discounts when purchased in bulk by corporations, organizations, and special-interest groups. For information, please e-mail orders@unitedhousepublishing.com

Dedicated to my wife Michelle and little girl Stella for all the love and support you have shown me over the years. To my parents who raised me to be my best and to always "remember who you are," in God's love. To our Love For A Child Kids Camp team for the dedication to help children in foster care. To my family and friends who have joined us on life's journey to make a lasting impact on families in need of hope. To Pastor Joe and Janet Wenturine for impacting my life at a young age when I was trying to find my purpose; I found it. For everyone who supports, sponsors, and—most of all—prays for the children who attend our camps to find comfort and true love in Jesus.

With Love,
Joe

A portion of the proceeds from the sale of *Little Joey Goes to Camp* goes directly to helping children in foster care.

Hi. My name is Little Joey!

I'm 6 years old, and let me tell you, there is no better place in the world than KIDS CAMP! It's a place where kids get to be kids and there is only one rule...

I'm a foster kid, which means I have had lots of different
people to call family and lots of different homes.
Every year, I go to summer camp with other kids who are just
like me. Camp is a safe place for my friends and me to go.

My job is to help my friends feel
WANTED and **WELCOME**
at camp.

My cabin is on the lake. In the morning,
the sun lights up the camp for all my friends,
the animals, and it makes the lake SHINE!

BOY'S CABIN

Every day is full of surprises for us, and most of the
activities we are doing will be for the first time **EVER!**

THE ROCKWALL IS AS TALL AS A MOUNTAIN!

It is a hard obstacle for little ol' me, but my friends always help me reach the top every time! I wouldn't trade this feeling for anything in the world! Don't let anyone ever tell you that you can't do something, even as a kid!

We get to go on a mud crawl and the girls have a princess tea party! We're all friends here but...

YUCK!

Other campers sometimes look at us like we're different, but if they got to know us, they would realize we are just like them. They may call us foster kids, but God calls us HIS AWESOME KIDS!

It doesn't matter what we've been through, or what we look like, at camp, we learn **WE ARE ALL CHILDREN OF GOD!**

They treat us like royalty here!

We eat all my favorite foods and desserts! The best part is all my friends eat like one big family for every meal. I never get to eat like this at home, but at camp, we eat and eat and eat and eat some more!

At night, we get to learn about super-cool Bible stories from our teacher, but before we start, I always bring him a very special gift!

Close your eyes,
SIT DOWN!

S'mores at night are always BIG
and extra gooey and...

CHOCOLATEY
& YUMMY!

CAMP is AMAZING!

I wish it would never end. The cross shines like a big nightlight in the sky!
At camp, they teach us that the cross will always keep us safe from harm's way and
out of trouble. If we focus on God's light, we won't be overlooked anymore. He will
always see us as His own. Goodnight friends! Goodnight Jesus! Thank you for everything.
I know whenever I whisper Your name, You're always right there next to me.

I love all my camp friends.

I know, with them by my side,
we will always be one
ROYAL FAMILY.

WE BELIEVE
KIDS SHOULD BE KIDS!

For let love be at the center of all we do. - 1 Corinthians 16:14 (paraphrased)

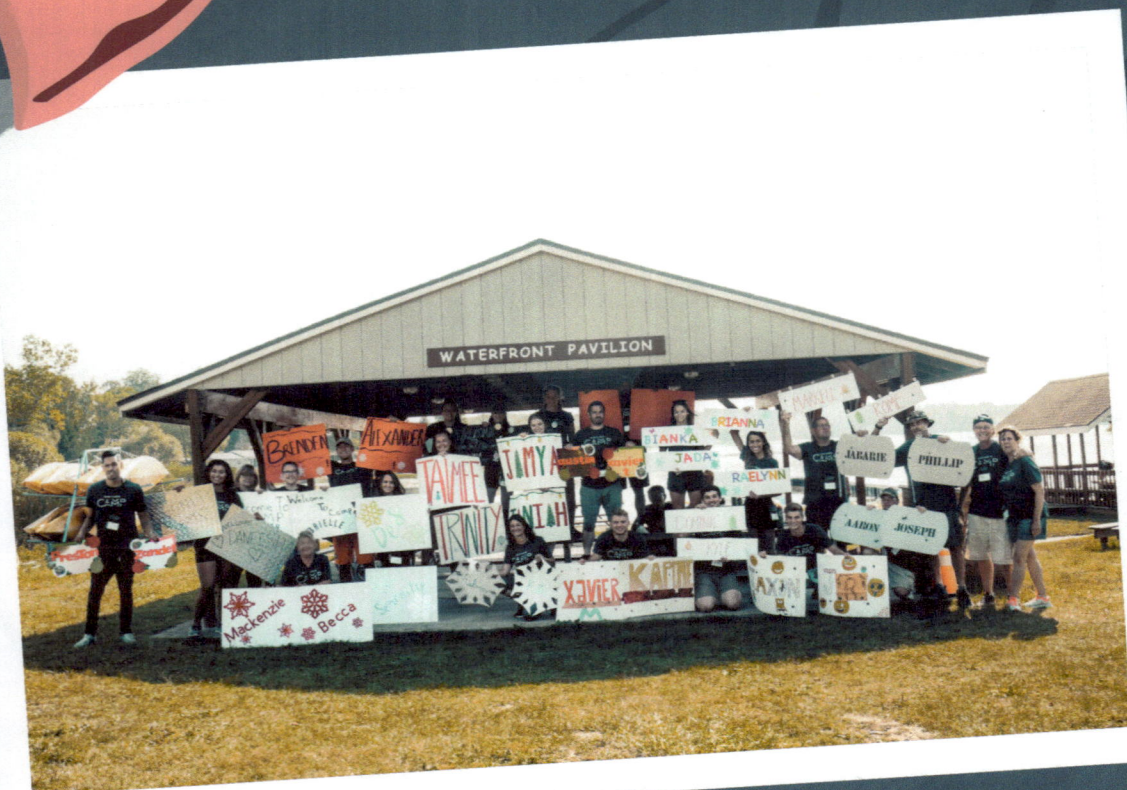

Love For A Child is an active 501c3 non-profit organization serving abused, abandoned, and neglected foster children. Our programs were created to help families in time of need; to provide resources and encouragement; and to remind everyone there is always hope in faith. Our mission is to reach the unreached, focus on the overlooked, and share our deepest compassion for families who are hoping someone will step in and offer a little help. Every year our program offers year-round mentoring, summer camps, and special moments for each child living in foster care. Michigan has a growing crisis for the development of children and youth living in the foster care system. We believe putting words into actions and making a difference.
For everything we do is authentically, whole-heartedly, Love for a Child.

To learn more or support this mission for foster care children, please visit **loveforachild.org**

JOE SAVALLE
Author of *Little Joey Goes to Camp*
Founder, Love for a Child

LITTLE JOEY

NATHAN BORTZ
Illustrator of *Little Joey Goes to Camp*

From the cozy small town shores of The Great Lakes State of Michigan, Joe Savalle is a children's author, humanitarian, and founder of the charity, Love for a Child. In *Little Joey Goes to Camp*, the character, known as "Little Joey", is derived from a real-life persona that Savalle created to teach children within foster care their value in life in a fun and lighthearted way. The Little Joey character has been teaching children for over a decade the meaning of happiness, joy in laughter, and that God will love us forever. Oh yeah, and he never leaves home without his whoopie cushion! Savalle, founder of Love for a Child Kids Camp, has dedicated his purpose and passion to teaching children who have had tough life situations that kids should be kids and that every child deserves a childhood worth remembering.

"To all the children out there in foster care, remember to live courageously, be brave, be a kid, and know that God's Love Never Fails."

- Joe Savalle

Nathan is a graphic designer by day and an illustrator by night; but, most importantly, a husband and father 'round the clock. Now more than ever, Nathan has a great appreciation for the pure and unencumbered enthusiasm for life that children can share with us, and he is forever grateful that he can revive this wonder in himself just by seeing the world through his son's eyes everyday.

May we all be curious, free to be brave, seeking knowledge, and open to compassion. Through the adversities of life, may we make it a point to reset and live through love.

www.ingramcontent.com/pod-product-compliance
Lightning Source LLC
Chambersburg PA
CBHW040406100426

42811CB00017B/1849